Believe in the power of *Necronomicon Spellbook* . . .

- A reader invoking the name of Ziku was blessed thereafter with extraordinary riches.
- After appealing to Namru, a college student went on to pass an important exam he was otherwise sure to fail.
- A police officer goes nowhere on patrol without the seal of Asarualimnunna concealed on his person.

These aren't the only extraordinary stories to come from the magick of these all-powerful spells.

Prove to yourself the strength and validity of these ancient words.

Work the miracles offered by the *Necronomicon*.

Books Written or Edited by
Simon

PAPAL MAGIC
THE GATES OF THE NECRONOMICON
DEAD NAMES
THE NECRONOMICON SPELLBOOK
THE NECRONOMICON

NECRONOMICON
SPELLBOOK

Edited by Simon

AVON BOOKS
An Imprint of HarperCollins*Publishers*

AVON BOOKS
An Imprint of HarperCollinsPublishers
10 East 53rd Street
New York, New York 10022-5299

Library of Congress Catalog Card Number: 86-64005
ISBN: 0-380-73112-6
www.avonbooks.com

First Avon Books printing: October 1998

Printed in the U.S.A.

21

THE CHURCH where it all began no longer exists. Like so much else in this bizarre case—which has been quietly making history in the last four years—it has receded silently into the mists of memory. Simon had been a monk, a priest, later an abbot and finally a consecrated bishop of this Eastern Church, becoming ordained even before he graduated high school. Coming from a Slavic background (his grandparents fled the Austro-Hungarian Empire) he acquired a broad knowledge of several foreign languages, including French, Spanish, Italian, Slavonic, Greek, Latin and even Mandarin Chinese. This ability enables him to communicate with people from many races and nationalities as well as to probe the mysteries of religion and magick in the ancient manuscripts and worn leather books from many long-forgotten lands. As a young priest, he found himself called upon to perform exorcisms among poor ethnic families in the sometimes seedy and dangerous New York City neighborhoods that were his parish. He had faced evil many times in his life, and battled with the devil himself in his many disguises. Yet, he was still not prepared for the sudden appearance of the NECRONOMICON that overcast afternoon in the Spring of 1972.

They had not quite made history yet, those two renegade monks who had unwittingly made it possible for Simon to be one of the first human beings to actually hold the notorious spellbook in his hands. But they would. Shortly thereafter, headlines in the **New York Times**, the **Christian Science Monitor** and other papers across the country proclaimed the awful truth. His two brother monks had been arrested for committing the biggest rare book heist in the history of the United States. Little did they know the true value of one of their ill-gotten possessions—the corroded box containing hundreds of pages of manuscript written in a large, cursive hand in the Greek tongue. It was only one of hundreds and hundreds more they had stolen from universities and private collections across the United States and Canada. The two monks would eventually serve time in a federal prison for their offense. And Simon would be left with the task of deciphering what appeared to be an ancient book of spells dating from the ninth century, A.D.

L. K. Barnes had been a student at the University of Colorado when he began painting the bizarre works of alien landscapes that have become his hallmark to all who know him now. Years ago, he had fantasized about finding the dread NECRONOMICON in an old used book shop, and many of his paintings and sculptures are of themes inspired by his voracious reading of Lovecraft's opus. Somehow, he knew the book had to exist. Somewhere. In some form. He knew it was not a mere fantasy of Lovecraft's—for the very concept of such a book held a power all its own. Then one day in 1977, a friend—whom we can identify only by his initials—B.A.K.—led him to the Magickal Childe Bookstore in Manhattan. It was just the type of strange and exotic place one would almost expect to find a NECRONOMICON stashed on a forgotten shelf. Jokingly, he asked the proprietor, Herman Slater, if such was the case.

"Certainly," he replied, and pulled Simon's translated manuscript from behind the counter. "Here it is."

The rest, as they say, is history.

Fighting against almost impossible odds, the first edition of the NECRONOMICON was published in December, 1977. Friends and business associates told both Simon and his new partner, L. K. Barnes, that the project was doomed to failure. That it was too expensive. That it would never sell. And that they would be stuck with a cursed book of evil magick for the rest of their lives. They were proven wrong. In a year, the first edition sold out even though it was retailing for fifty dollars a copy. In less than a year, the equally expensive second edition was sold out and a third edition was just printed in 1981. The paperback rights were sold, and there has been talk of motion picture rights for the story of the NECRONOMICON.

But the emergence of the NECRONOMICON has

spawned a whole generation of imitations since 1977. The brilliant artist and creator of the sets for the movie **Alien**—H. R. Giger—has come out with his own **Necronomicon:** a series of paintings based loosely on the subterranean concepts of H. P. Lovecraft, who popularized the book in the 1920s and 1930s through his short stories and novellas, depicting the NECRONOMICON as the most blasphemous and sinister book of spells the world has ever known (an attitude no doubt based on a serious misunderstanding of the book's true origins and purpose). The British author, Colin Wilson, collaborated in a thin volume published in 1978 containing speculation concerning the existence of the NECRONOMICON. Stephen Skinner mentioned it in his introduction to the **Enochian Dictionary**, and Francis King has mentioned it in his introduction to the **Armadel**—a reprint of a spell book of the Middle Ages.

A reviewer for **Fate** Magazine warned his readers against possible misuse of the Book as it might involve serious hazards to one's health (mental, physical, or spiritual?), and indeed much of the Book's legend concerns the formulae for the invocation of dark powers from under the earth or beyond the veil of the stars. However, **these same forces are in actuality no more than the long-forgotten psychic abilities of humanity**, retained over millions of years since the first human walked the earth and was in intimate communication with the powers of nature, the heavens, and the animal kingdom. These forces are the remnants of ancient gods worshipped by the earliest recorded Western civilization: the Sumerians—a race that disappeared mysteriously from the face of the earth over four thousand years ago.

The Editor and Publishers of the NECRONOMICON hope, by this volume, to present a short guide to the use of the spells of the Book that would enable anyone to simply pick it up and use it without fear or risk. The spells concerning the Fifty Names of the Sumerian God Marduk were chosen because of their universal appeal to the basic needs and desires of every human being; Love, Wealth, Peace of Mind, Protection Against Enemies, and Wisdom being among them. The

Editor felt that the benefits to be derived from the use of these spells should not be restricted to those who have the time and the academic background necessary to follow the entire complex system through to its end: a process that would take most people over a year to perform properly. Instead, in the following pages, a simple method of using the names, words and seals of Marduk has been outlined and demonstrated so that anyone can follow the process easily and with success.

This means you.

We have received many letters from people who have been very impressed with our publication of the **NECRONOMICON** but who find the arcane language and eerie instructions and diagrams a trifle confusing, and who have asked us to simplify it for them so that they could get right into the spells and turn their lives around—without entailing any psychic harm. We have seen it as our responsibility, therefore, to present this book as an answer to those letters and those requests for a neat, simple method of using the ancient and awe-some forces of the NECRONOMICON to gain wisdom, power, love and protection in these troubled times.

So, we urge you not to put off using the spells that make up half of this report. There is no reason why you should sit back and wait for someone else to pick it up and later tell you how great it worked, how wonderful the results are, how fast your wishes can come true. This is **your** opportunity to decide that finally, today, you assume full and total responsibility for your life and happiness; that the time for sorrow, fear, doubt and confusion is over; that from now on, you are your own master with the help of the magick of the incredible NECRONOMICON.

THESE SPELLS were originally worked by the mystics of ancient Sumeria—a mysterious civilization that flourished in what is now known as Iraq over two thousand years before the birth of Christ. No one knows who the Sumerians really were, or where they came from. Some say they came from the darkest parts of

Africa, where they were a nomadic people. Then, suddenly, in less than a hundred years they became a full-fledged agricultural society with cities and farms and beautiful temples that reached to the skies. They gave credit for their awakening to a strange being who came to them from the sea, wearing a diving suit, and who taught them writing, science, agriculture, architecture and, of course, magick. Almost overnight, the Sumerians became a people. Working the system of the NECRONOMICON in their seven-storied temples, they became the most cultured and powerful force in the Middle East. It is their system of magick that has been retained in the NECRONOMICON. Now, after literally thousands of years, this secret mystical system for winning power, love and success is made available to everyone.

Of course, the original spells were in the Sumerians' own language, but thanks to the team of translators who worked with Simon on the decipherment of the manuscript, we can now understand what the spells were about and how to work them properly in English.

But, in order to work properly, some Sumerian words have been kept because they are known as "words of power." A "word of power" is a word that contains power in itself; in its very pronunciation, in the sounds that comprise it. It cannot be changed, or else its power would be lost forever. Hence, we have kept the original Sumerian words of power in their original state, with the sounds intact. Some of them may look difficult to pronounce at first, but take it very slowly and you will derive much benefit from it. These are the words once spoken thousands of years ago in the Sumerian temples to summon cosmic forces of such scope that the mind clearly balks at trying to picture the rituals that must have accompanied them in those days. So take the time and trouble to learn the correct way to pronounce the words you want to use. The effort will pay off a hundredfold when you actually employ your ritual.

STEP ONE

Once you have found the spell you wish to use from the following seals and descriptions, make a copy of the seal on fresh, clean paper with black ink. You make the seal as large or small as you wish. Keep it in a safe place until you are ready to use it, and never—under any circumstances—let another person look at it before or after you use it. It is for your eyes only.

STEP TWO

Choose a quiet evening and a place where you will not be disturbed for your ritual. The best time is about three in the morning, when distractions (both natural and psychic) are at their lowest intensity. Have your seal ready in front of you. Light two white candles and place them at either side of the seal on a table or desk. If you care to, light a stick of incense. Pine or sandalwood is best, or cedar. The Moon should be waxing, but in cases of emergency this is not necessary. Any time will do. When this has all been arranged, sit quietly for a few minutes and think about the goal you want to achieve.

STEP THREE

While looking intently at the seal you have made—so that it is the only thing you can see—take three deep breaths, slowly, one at a time. Concentrate on the goal at the same time, seeing it as a picture if possible. A picture of yourself sitting in a pile of cash, or with your arms around a loved one, or within a protective circle. Then, slowly raise your eyes—without lifting your head—to the heavens and say, slowly and clearly:

ZI KIA KANPA.

(Zee-Kee-Ya-Kan-Pa)

ZI ANNA KANPA.

(Zee-An-Na-Kan-Pa)

ZI DINGIR KIA KANPA.

(Zee-Deen-Geer-Kee-Ya-Kan-Pa)

ZI DINGIR ANNA KANPA.

(Zee-Deen-Geer-An-Na-Kan-Pa)

Hear me, O Thou ____________

(here insert the Name of the Spirit you are invoking)

Come to Me by the

Powers of the Word ____________

(here insert the word of the Spirit you are invoking)

And answer my urgent prayer!

ZI KIA KANPA!

ZI ANNA KANPA!

STEP FOUR

Then slowly lower your eyes back to the seal in front of you and stare intently at the drawing, at the same time forming a clear mental image of the end you are trying to achieve. Do not pay any attention to any strange or eerie feelings you may experience at this point. They are common with this type of ritual and are no cause for alarm. It is important that you do not break concentration for any purpose whatsoever, so ignore the odd sounds and sensations that *might* accompany the performance of any of these rituals. They are simply the weak attempts of unevolved psychic entities trying to disrupt your ritual. They are not worthy of your attention.

STEP FIVE

When you have passed a few moments this way, and you feel your concentration beginning to wane, then close the ritual with the following prayer:

—ZI DINGIR KIA KANPA.
(Zee-Deen-Geer-Kee-Ya-Kan-Pa)
ZI DINGIR ANNA KANPA
(Zee-Deen-Geer-An-Na-Kan-Pa)
Spirit of the Earth, Remember!
Spirit of the Sky, Remember!

Take three more deep breaths, then stand up (if you have been sitting), and walk a few steps around the room looking at all the objects that might be there: furniture, pictures, etc. and touch a few of these objects. This serves two purposes—one: it helps to solidify your astral body if the preceding ritual has caused it to become overly sensitive to passing vibrations, making it weak and vulnerable, and two: it distracts the conscious mind from the basically *unconscious* process that the ritual has just begun. Now, return to the table on which your seal has been placed.

STEP SIX

Take the seal you have just made and cover it, or turn it over, or put it away somewhere where no one will see it. The seal has been *charged*, in a subtle way, and now can no longer be used for any other purpose except what it was consecrated to do in your ritual. *You must not use the same seal twice for different goals*, although you may use it twice for the same goal, in case you wish to repeat your ritual the following night. It is best not to repeat it for more than three consecutive nights for reasons it would be too complicated to explain here. Extinguish the candles and place them where you will find them easily for your next ritual. They can be used again for any ritual, but must never be used for simply lighting the room. Once used in a ritual from the NECRONOMICON, they can be used for no other purpose save a similar ritual from the NECRONOMICON. Do not use these candles for other rituals (that is, from other spellbooks) or for any mundane purpose. You must take these rituals quite seriously, and treat the tools you use in a ritual with the same respect a carpenter has for his saw and hammer, or a plumber for his wrench or a priest for his Bible. In a way, by using these rituals, you have become a kind of priest or priestess yourself, for you have joined a select order of initiates that has been practicing these and similar mystical rituals since the beginning of recorded history.

STEP SEVEN (OPTIONAL)

Most of our readers and students have found it enormously valuable to keep a written record of all rituals they perform, so that they can easily assess what their results are by using any particular ritual or spell. They can gauge how long it will take for a certain spell to work, and also they can refresh their memory in the future with accounts of all the successes they have enjoyed through using the NECRONOMICON. The first time a spell works, you may want to believe it's only a coincidence. But later, as time goes by and more and more of your spells are working—with phenomenal results—it's good to go back and look through your magickal diary to see just how wrong you were about coincidence and to prove to yourself once and for all that, yes, magick does work!

BEFORE YOU go straight to the Names, a few words of information.

According to Sumerian mythology, Marduk was the God who defeated the Ancient Ones long before the creation of matter as we know it. Against him in battle were the fierce TIAMAT, KINGU and AZAGTHOTH. Once he had destroyed these demons, he created the universe from the flesh of TIAMAT, and humanity from the blood of KINGU mixed with his own breath. You will come across these names in the description of the Fifty Names, which were titles given to Marduk by the Elder Gods after he had helped them to defeat the Ancient Ones. This is nothing less than the Biblical story of the war in heaven and the fall of Lucifer; and, in fact, it was recorded by the Sumerians even before there was a Jewish religion, as the Sumerians were the first civilization in the Middle East and their holy books and legends became the basis for much that we read in the Old Testament. The Tower of Babel, for instance, is very probably the Ziggurat (or temple) of Babylon, which was originally a Sumerian city before it was captured by the Assyrian hordes.

Several of the Names do not have Words. In that case, the Fifty Names are given in the section entitled "A Guide to the Spells."

The special Seal for each Name is given on the chart.

I.
The First Name is MARDUK.

The Lord of Lords, Master of Magicians. His name should not be called except when no other will do, and it is the most terrible responsibility to do so. The word of his calling is DUGGA.

This, the first name of MARDUK, should only be used when life is threatened. It is not wise to use it on any other occasion, or flippantly in any way. To do so would be to render the other seals and names worthless, for MARDUK would abandon you to your fate.

2.
The Second Name is MARUKKA.

Knows all things since the beginning of the World. Knows all secrets, be they human or divine, and is very difficult to summon. The Priest should not summon him unless he is clean of heart and spirit, for this Spirit shall know his innermost thoughts.

The warning should, of course, be taken seriously. Can be useful in an emergency situation when the knowledge of some secret thing is important to life or limb, but a time of purification should be observed at any rate after the Spirit is summoned. There is no word for this spirit. It must be summoned by the force of your desire.

3.

The Third Name is Marutukku.

Master of the Arts of Protection, chained the Mad God at the Battle. Sealed the Ancient Ones in their Caves, behind the Gates. Possesses the ARRA star.

To be used especially when performing any occult ceremony in which there is danger, such as the invocation of demonic forces. The ARRA star is a five-pointed Pentagram, and is the universal symbol of protection. Protects the soul as well as the body.

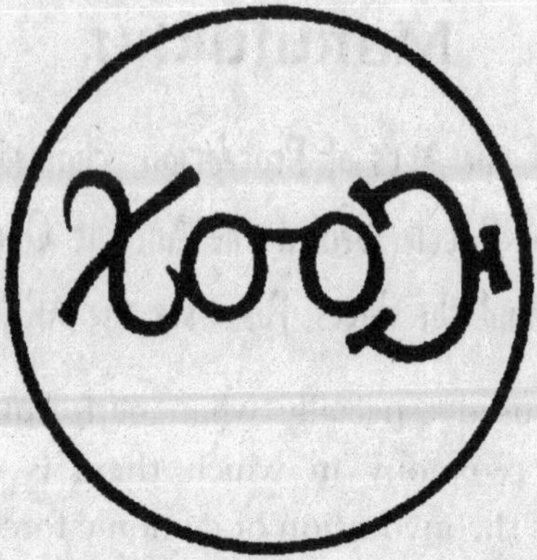

4.
The Fourth Name is Barashakushu.

Worker of Miracles. The kindest of the Fifty, and the most beneficent. The Word used at his Calling is BAALDURU.

Can be used in hopeless cases, when it seems that the whole world is against you or a loved one. When despair reaches its lowest depth, and a coldness constricts your soul, call forcefully upon BARASHAKUSHU with all your might and hope and your prayer will be answered in ways you cannot imagine.

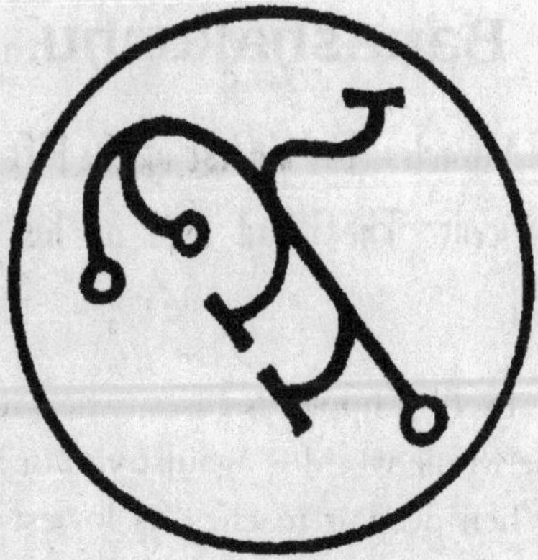

5.
The Fifth Name is LUGGALDIMMERANKIA.

Puts order into CHAOS. Made the Waters aright. Commander of Legions of Wind Demons who fought the Ancient TIAMAT alongside MARDUK KURIOS. The word used at his Calling is BANUTUKKU.

This seal has proven useful when confusion has taken hold of the mind and no way can be seen to end the mess a life is in. To sharpen your perception of a problem and to discover a hidden answer—one you have constantly overlooked—call upon this spirit and a cloud will lift from your heart and mind and the solution to an important problem will reveal itself in all its simplicity.

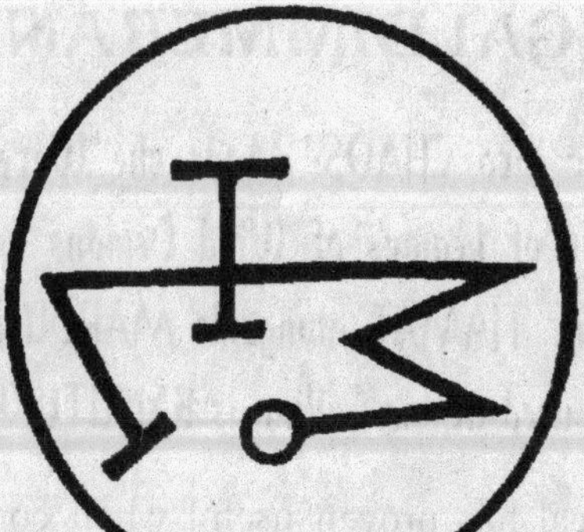

6.

The Sixth Name is NARILUGGAL-DIMMERANKIA.

The Watcher of the IGIGI and the ANNUNAKI. Sub-Commander of the Wind Demons. He will put to flight any maskim who haunt thee, and is the foe of the rabisu. None may pass into the World Above or the World Below without his knowledge. His word is BANRABISHU.

A good Spirit for warding off feelings of aggravation and irritation, as well as the gnawing feelings of dread that sometimes come in the wee hours of the morning, when you feel lost and alone. Merely the pronunciation of the Word BANRABISHU at these times is sufficient to dispel most of these negative emotions. To be said with force and strength in the four directions.

7.
The Seventh Name is ASARULUDU.

Wielder of the Flaming Sword, oversees the Race of Watchers at the bidding of the Elder Gods. He ensures the most perfect safety, especially in dangerous tasks undertaken at the behest of the Astral Gods, his Word is BANMASKIM.

Like the Angel in Genesis, this Spirit protects a place, a home or temple, from negative psychic and magickal attacks. Like the Sixth Spirit, merely the pronunciation of his Word BANMASKIM is sufficient to dispel hostile influences when shouted to the four quarters. Maskim and Rabisu are the names of ancient Sumerian demons.

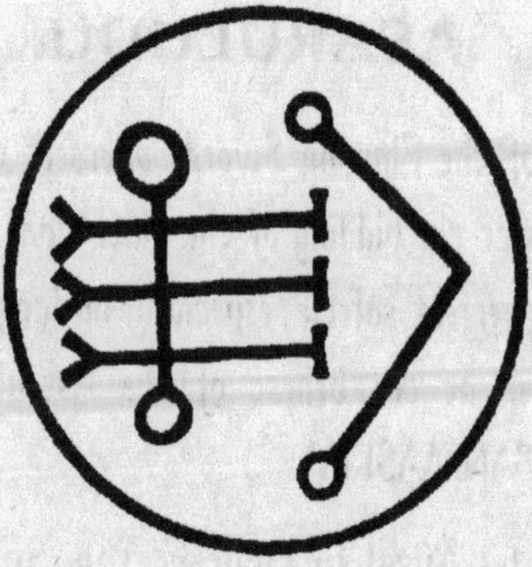

8.
The Eighth Name is NAMTILLAKU.

A most secret and potent Lord, he hath knowledge to raise the dead and conserve with the spirits of the Abyss, unbenownst to their Queen. No soul passes into Death but that he is aware. His word is BANU-TUKUKUTUKKU.

Similar to Lord Yama of the Tibetans or Baron Samedi of the Voudoun cult, this spirit has the power to see beyond the veil that separates the living from the dead and can reveal secrets that have been carried to the grave.

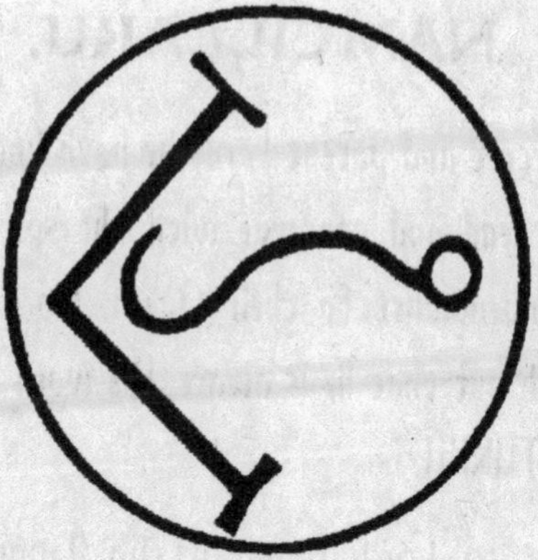

9.
The Ninth Name is NAMRU.

Dispenses wisdom and knowledge in all things. Giveth excellent counsel and teaches the science of metals. His Word is BAKAKLAMU.

One reader writes to us and says "Although I am excellent in most of my subjects at (a college on the East Coast), I am a general failure at science. It was then that I got a copy of your NECRONOMICON and my eyes fell to the seal of NAMRU. I prayed the night before an important Chemistry midterm exam to NAMRU and carried his seal into the classroom. I passed a test I thought I would never even get a 35 in with an astonishing 85. Suddenly, it just seemed that I understood the subject for the first time in my life."

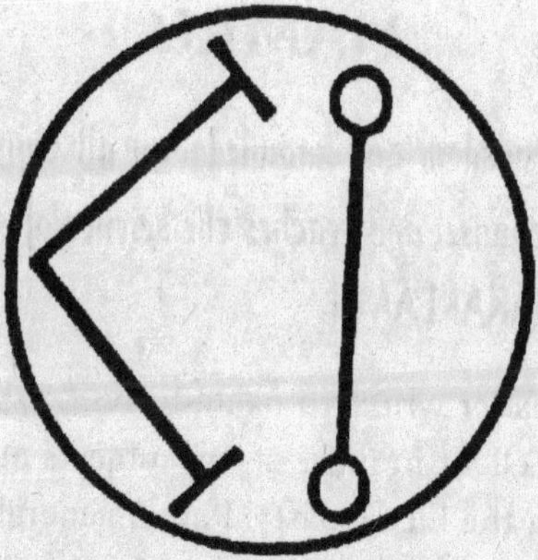

10.
The Tenth Name is ASARU.

This Power has knowledge of all plants and trees, and can make marvellous fruits to grow in the desert places, and no land is a waste to him. He is truly the Protector of the Bounty. His word is BAALPRIKU.

The application of the powers of this Spirit is obvious. Can be used for a simple window box flower, or an entire farm, to protect against blight and drought, and to insure a bountiful harvest.

11.
The Eleventh Name is Asarualim.

Possesses secret wisdom, and shines Light in the Darkened areas, forcing what lives there to give good accounting of its existence and its knowledge. Gives excellent counsel in all things. His word is BAR-RMARATU.

For those who dabble in the necromantic arts, or who are involved with spiritualism, santeria, voodoo, macumba, or any of the other arts which deal of communication with invisible spirits and gods, this Spirit is a tester and measurer of their truth. Can protect one from being deceived by negative or unruly spirits, or by those who seek to convince you that they are in communication with those forces when, in truth, they are not. When engraved in metal and worn on the person in the presence of deception, the metal has a tendency to get warm to the touch.

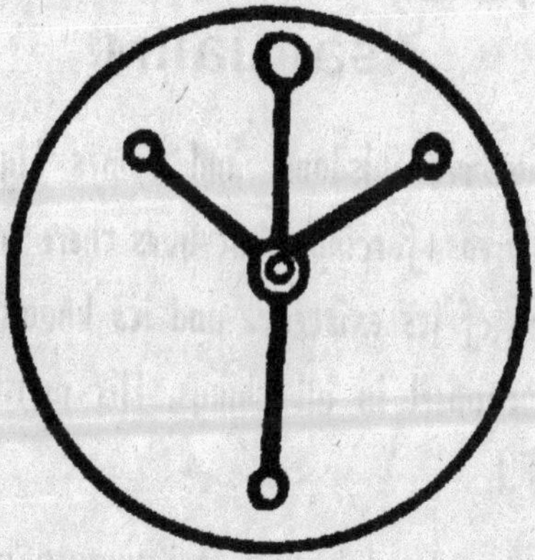

12.

The Twelfth Name is ASARUALIMNUNNA.

This is the power that presideth over armor of all kinds and is excellently knowledgeable in military matters, being of the advance army of MARDUK at that Battle. He can provide an army with its entire weaponry in three days. His Word is BANATATU.

An Auxiliary Police officer of our acquaintance goes nowhere on patrol without the seal of this spirit concealed on his clothing.

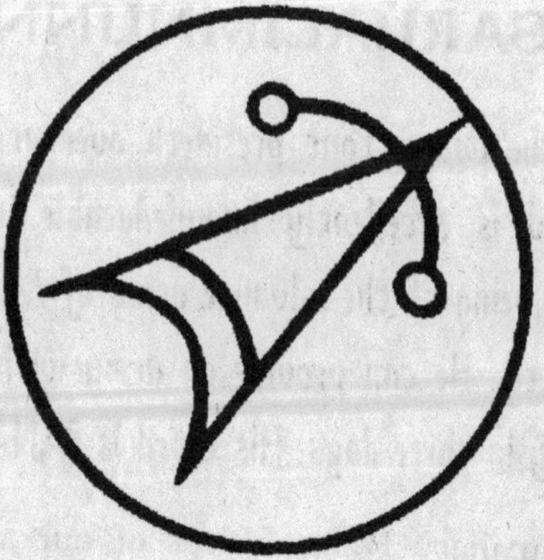

13.

The Thirteenth Name is TUTU.

Silences the weeping and gives joy to the sad and ill at heart. A most beneficent Name, and Protector of the Household, his word is DIRRIGUGIM.

Sadness can sometimes be a heavy burden and a negative emotion that eats away at our body and soul as surely as any disease. Quite often, only a change of perspective is needed to quell the soul's trembling. A kind word, a sympathetic ear, a knowing intelligence, the hand of friendship. Those who call on this spirit find an unspeakable peace descends on their souls and lightens their spirits so that they can return to the world of the living with a sense of relief and renewed faith in themselves and the world. Can be summoned to aid a friend in distress as well as to give yourself a much-needed sense of joy and well-being.

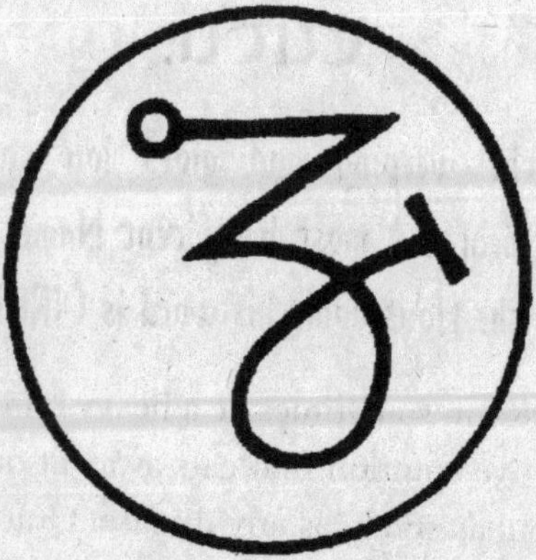

14.

The Fourteenth Name is ZIUKKINNA.

Giveth excellent knowledge concerning the movements of the stars and the meanings thereof, of which the Chaldeans possessed this same knowledge in abundance. The Word is GIBBILANNU.

An excellent patron Spirit for astrologers and astronomers, and a good aid for those who read the sacred TAROT as well. The psychic abilities of astrologers who use the ZIUKKINNA in their workings will become greatly expanded.

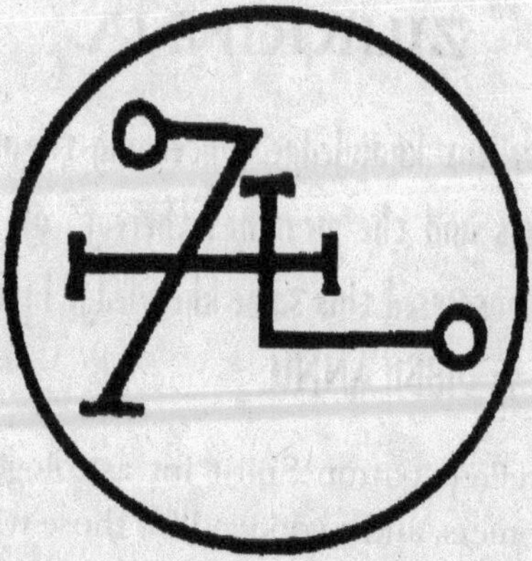

15.
The Fifteenth Name is ZIKU.

This power bestoweth Riches of all kinds and can tell where treasure is hidden. Knower of the Secrets of the Earth. His Word is GIGGIMAGANPA.

Although quite often scholars attribute metaphorical meanings to the powers said to be found in spiritual spellbooks, ZIKU has been known to work both ways: literal and metaphorical. A reader who has used ZIKU before writes to tell us that after invoking him she discovered a ten-dollar bill in the street. That was only the beginning, however. She discovered that her attic contained a valuable stamp collection that she sold to an interested buyer the following week. A "hidden treasure?"

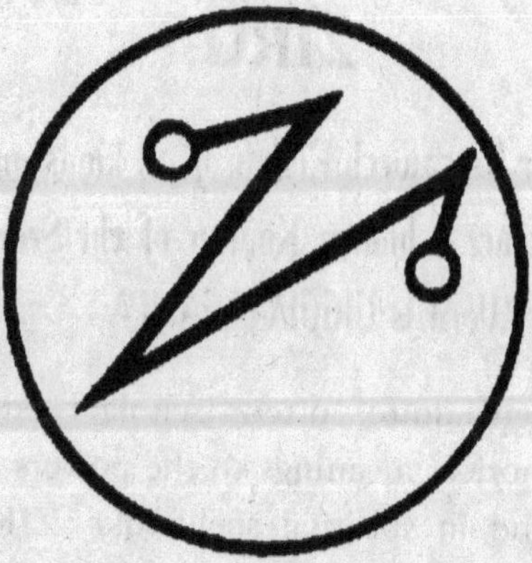

16.
The Sixteenth Name is AGAKU.

This Power can give life to what is already dead, but for a short time only. He is the Lord of the AMULET and the TALISMAN. His word is MASHGARZANNA.

Some explanation is necessary to understand the full implications of AGAKU. The bestowing of life into dead objects is a specialty of those magicians who deal in TALISMANIC magick. In this ART, a drawing or engraving is made of some occult symbol that represents a goal to be achieved (to make an extreme case, drawing a dollar sign on a piece of paper to represent money or wealth). This "talisman" must then be consecrated and give "life," which is the life-force and True Will of the magician transmitted to the Talisman. AGAKU can assist the budding magician by expediting this transfer of life-force to the talisman.

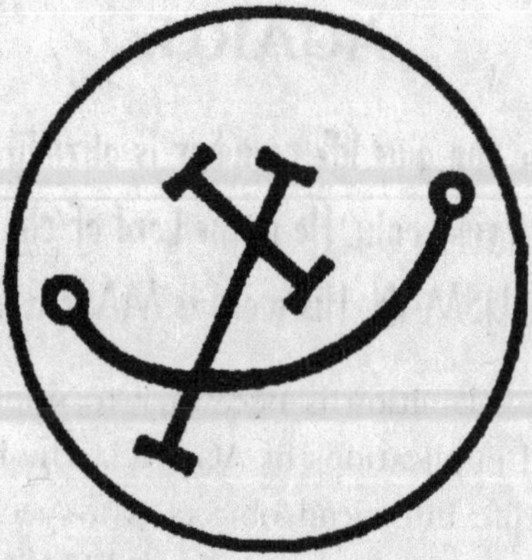

17.
The Seventeenth Name is TUKU.

Lord of Baneful Magick, Vanquisher of the Ancient Ones by Magick, giver of the Spell to MARDUK KURIOS, a most fierce enemy. His Word is MASHSHAMMASHTI.

There are times when we feel that someone else may be practicing magick against us. The feeling is hard to describe to anyone else, but we know it when it happens. If you are certain that magick is being used against you, that a spell has been cast or a curse sent in your direction, then the name and seal of this spirit will repel the evildoer as surely as if Archangel Michael had been summoned to rout Lucifer from Heaven. A most potent protection device.

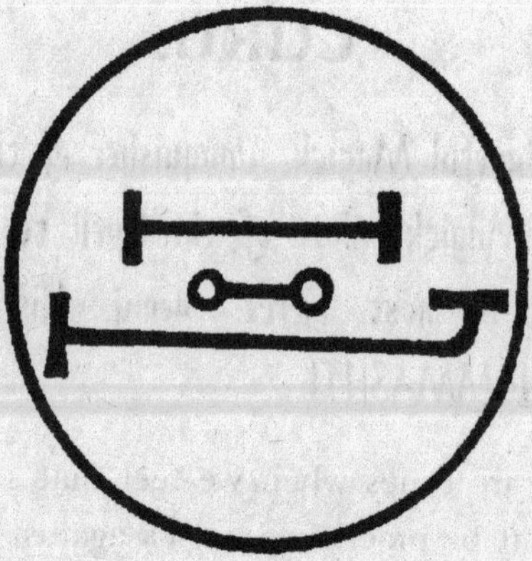

18.
The Eighteenth Name is SHAZU.

Knows the thoughts of those at a distance, as well as those in the vicinity. Nothing is buried in the ground, or thrown into the water, but this Power is aware. His Word is MASHSHANANNA.

Can assist the magician in developing powers of telepathy and ESP, as well as the special abilities of divination (telling past and future, as well as present, events through the use of the Tarot cards, the I Ching, or any of the thousands of methods in use since time began).

19.
The Nineteenth Name is ZISI.

Reconciler of enemies, silencer of arguments, between two people or between two nations, or even, it is said, between two worlds. The scent of Peace is indeed sweet to this Power, whose word is MASHINANNA.

The function of this Spirit is obvious by the above description. Can heal a lover's quarrel, a marital spat, a lawsuit, or even greater problems. These Fifty Names of MARDUK are from the original Battle that divided the universe into Good and Evil, and hence the forces they represent are primal and hearken back to a time before recorded history, before the collective memory of humanity.

20.
The Twentieth Name is SUHRIM.

Seeks out the Worshippers of the Ancient Ones wherever they may be. The Priest who sends him on an errand does so at terrible risk, for SUHRIM kills easily, and without thought. His Word is MASSHANGERGAL.

We will not comment on the above.

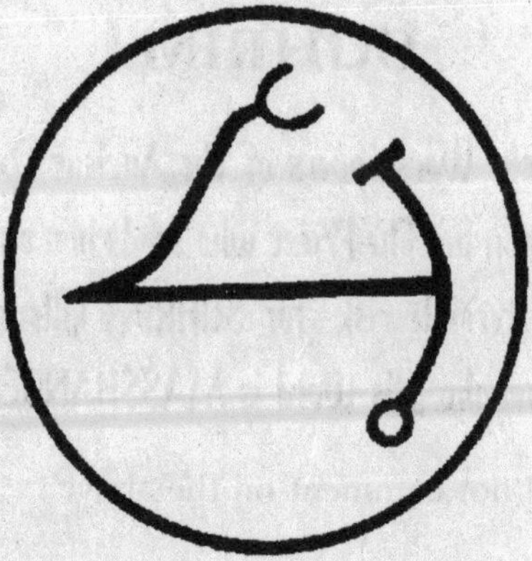

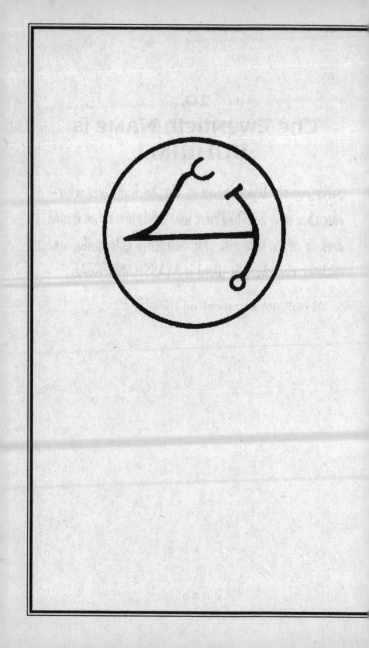

21.
The Twenty-First Name is SUHGURIM.

As SUHRIM before, the Foe who Cannot be Appeased. Discovers the Priest's Enemies with ease, but must be cautioned not to slay them if the Priest does not desire it. The Word is MASHSHADAR.

Again, we refuse to comment, except to say that to use either SUHRIM or SUHGURIM, as with ZAHRIM and ZAHGURIM, is a dangerous act of perhaps questionable morality. Magick was worked hard in this tradition.

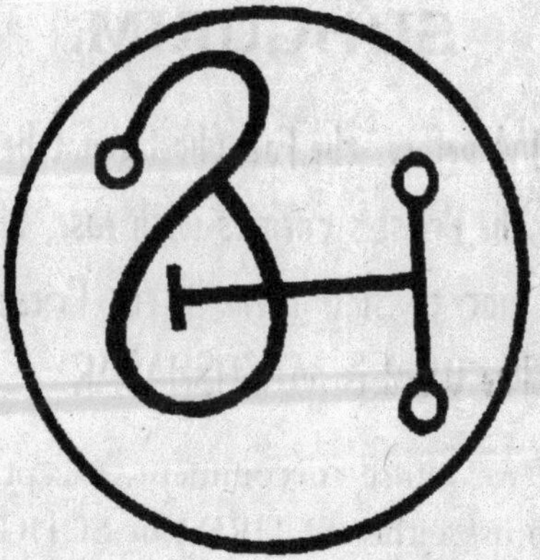

22.
The Twenty-Second Name is ZAHRIM.

Slew ten thousand of the Hordes in the Battle. A Warrior among Warriors. Can destroy an entire army if the Priest so desires. His Word is MASHSHA-GARANNU.

See pages 60-61.

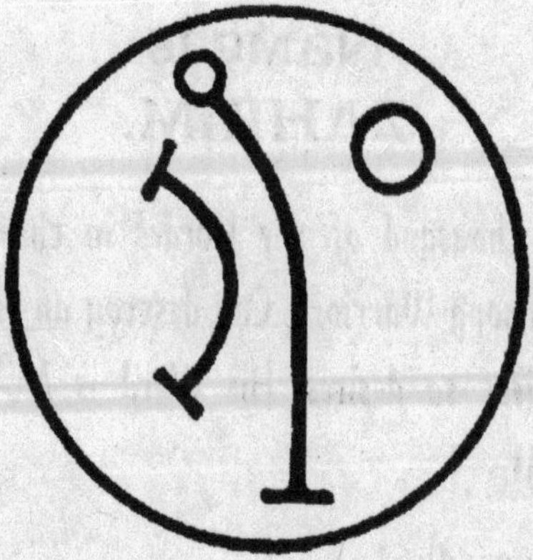

23.

The Twenty-Third Name is ZAHGURIM.

As ZAHRIM, a most terrible opponent. It is said ZAHGURIM slays slowly, after a most unnatural fashion. I do not know, for I have never summoned this Spirit. It is thy risk. The Word is MASHTISHADDU.

Right.

24.

The Twenty-Fourth Name is ENBILULU.

This Power can seek out water in the midst of a desert or on the tops of mountains. Knows the Secrets of Water, and the running of rivers below the Earth. A most useful Spirit. His Word is MASHSHANEBBU.

For irrigation, drought, dowsing, "Most useful."

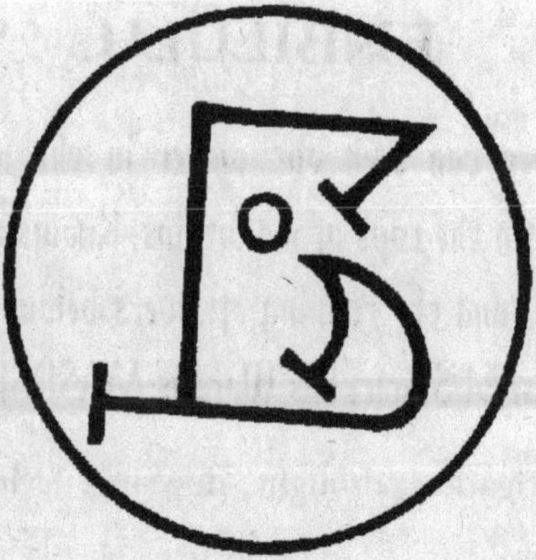

25.
The Twenty-Fifth Name is EPADUN.

This is the Lord of all Irrigation and can bring Water from a far place to your feet. Possesses a most subtle geometry of the Earth and knowledge of all lands where Water might be found in abundance. His Word is EYUNGINAKANPA.

The use of EPADUN is obvious by the preceding sentences. Water is fast becoming a scarce commodity in some areas of the earth, and dowsers are often called in to help locate sources of water under the ground. How much more powerful they could be with knowledge of the power of the NECRONOMICON and the Sumerian spirit called EPADUN.

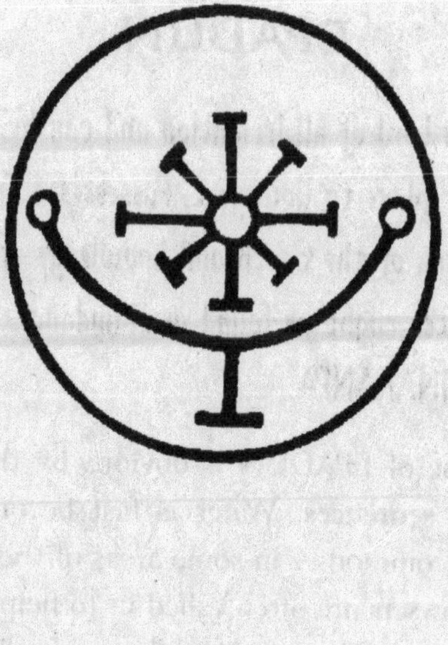

26.

The Twenty-Sixth Name is ENBILULUGUGAL.

The Power that presides over all growth, and all that grows. Gives knowledge of cultivation, and can supply a starving city with food for thirteen moons in one moon. A most noble Power. His Word is AGGHA.

Scientist predict a world-wide famine in twenty years.

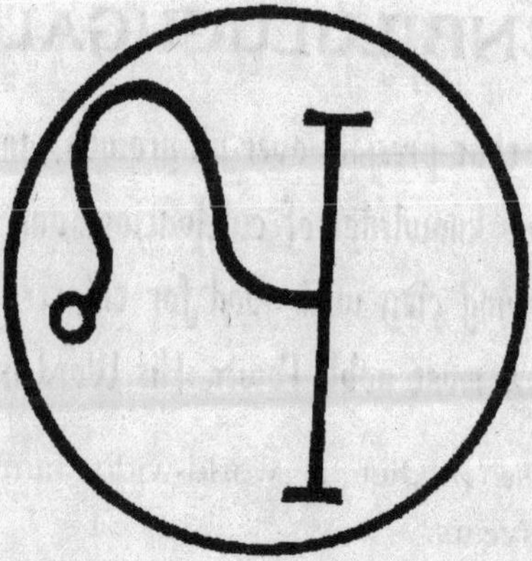

27.
The Twenty-Seventh Name is HEGAL.

As the Power above, a Master of the arts of farming and agriculture. Bestows rich harvests. Possesses the knowledge of the metals of the earth, and of the plough. His Word is BURDISHU.

An accomplished mystic writes to us to say that another ability of this Spirit is in the realm of sexual reproduction in people as well, and asserts that HEGAL can reveal secrets concerning human sexuality and fertility, linking HEGAL with the Semitic Spirit HAGIEL, a Spirit of the planet Venus.

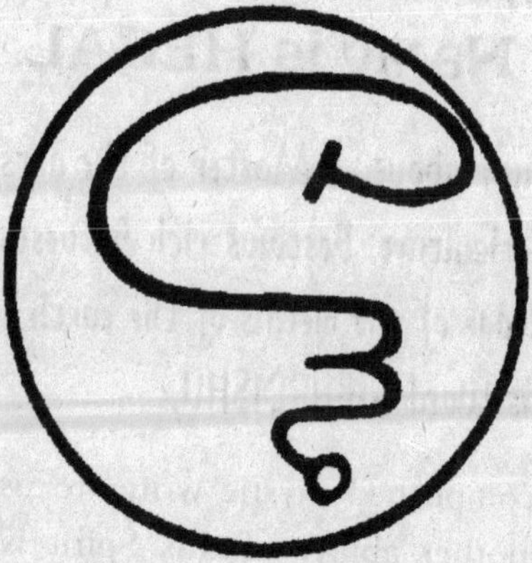

28.
The Twenty-Eighth Name is SIRSIR.

The Destroyer of TIAMAT, hated of the Ancient Ones, Master over the Serpent, Foe of KUTULU. A most powerful Lord. His Word is APIRIKUBA-BADAZUZUKANPA.

A secret application of this Spirit concerns celibacy and the harnessing of the sexual urge for greater magickal power, as is done in some Western and Eastern occult traditions.

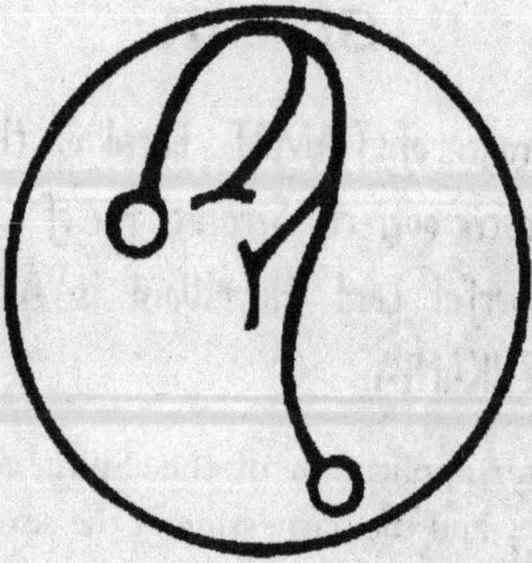

29.
The Twenty-Ninth Name is MALAH.

Trod the back of the Worm and cut it in twain. Lord of Bravery and Courage, and gives these qualities to the Priest who desires it, or to others the Priest may decide. The Word is BACHACHADUGG.

One of the prime characteristics of survivors is an inner sense of courage in the face of near impossible odds. Quite often, all that stands between us and success is the courage to do the right thing. Self-confidence does not come with being born. It must be learned. MALAH can help. The use of this seal and name acts within days—some say within minutes—to instill an exhilarating feeling of superiority. One feels equal to any task, no matter how hard or forbidding.

30.
The Thirtieth Name is GIL.

The Furnisher of Seed. The Beloved of ISHTAR, his Power is mysterious and quite ancient. Makes the barley to grow and the women to give birth. Makes potent the impotent. His Word is AGGABAL.

No further comment is necessary.

31.
The Thirty-First Name is GILMA.

Founder of cities, Possessor of the Knowledge of Architecture by which the fabled temples of UR were built; the creator of all that is permanent and never moves. His Word is AKABAL.

Also reveals the hidden structure in all things, from the tiniest molecule or atom to the solar system, galaxy, universe. Can show you the Pattern of any event or object, can reveal the love triangle as well as the golden triangle of the geometers. Aids students at the university as easily as the children in a kindergarten class studying the names for the colors.

32.
The Thirty-Second Name is AGILMA.

Bringer of Rain. Maketh the gentle Rains to come, or causeth great Storms and Thunders, the like may destroy armies and cities and crops. His Word is MASHSHAYEGURRA.

The supply of potable water is becoming an increasing problem in many countries. Many magicians have made their fortunes simply on the ability to provide rain to parched towns and farmland. Another Spirit whose usefulness will become more and more apparent as the next few years go by.

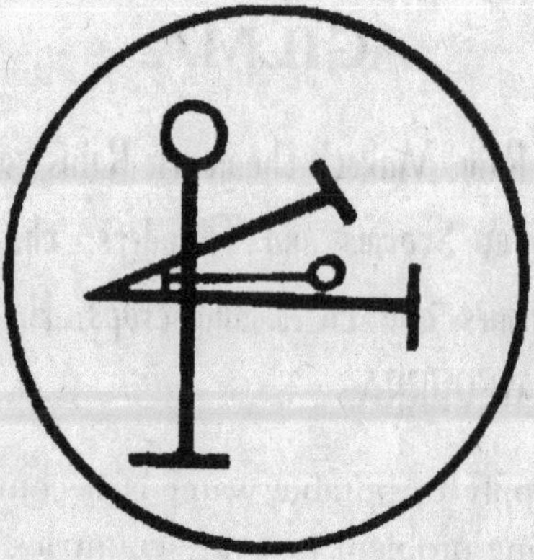

33.
The Thirty-Third Name is ZULUM.

Knows where to plant and when to plant. Giveth excellent counsel in all manner of business and commerce. Protects a man from evil tradesmen. His word is ABBABAAL.

Certainly a practical force, ZULUM's abilities range from aiding a person in the development of a green thumb to advising a person in the management of a multinational corporation. Can protect your store or home against conmen and frauds. Invoke daily whenever involved in a particularly sticky or important business deal with people you don't particularly trust.

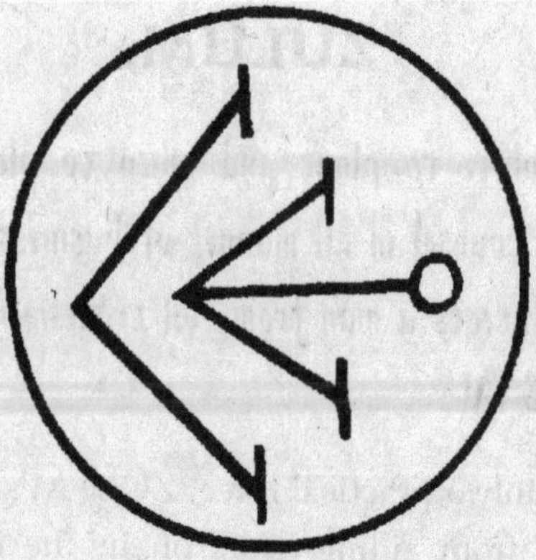

34.

The Thirty-Fourth Name is MUMMU.

The Power given to MARDUK to fashion the universe from the flesh of TIAMAT. Giveth wisdom concerning the condition of life before the creation, and the nature of the structures of the Four Pillars whereupon the Heavens rest. His Word is ALALALABAAAL.

Before there was Matter according to certain mystics—there was only Energy. This Spirit is summoned to impart knowledge of this divine and cosmic fire to the magickal aspirant.

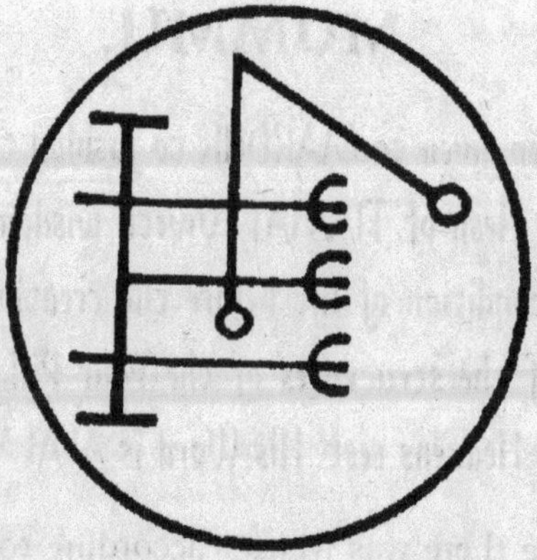

35.

The Thirty-Fifth Name is ZULUMMAR.

Giveth tremendous strength, as of ten men, to one man. Lifted the part of TIAMAT that was to become the Sky from the part that was to become the Earth. His Word is ANNDARABAAL.

Continued evocation of this Spirit over a period of several weeks will increase vitality and vigor in the weak and sickly. It will add lustre to the health and strength of the strong.

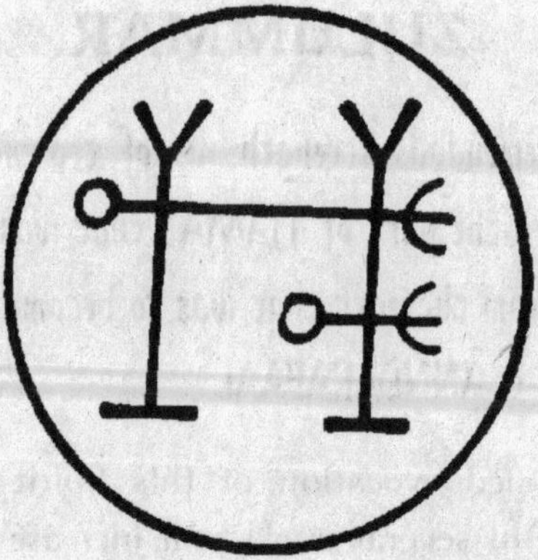

36.
The Thirty-Sixth Name is LUGALABDUBUR.

Destroyer of the Gods of TIAMAT. Vanquisher of Her Hordes. Chained KUTULU to the Abyss. Fought AZAGTHOTH with skill. A great Defender and a great Attacker. His Word is AGNIBAAL.

A Spirit to increase one's sense of self, or confidence and self-assurance, by working on speeding up the reactions—mental and physical—that determine our behavior. Gives the agility of a fencer and the acuity of a chessplayer. Also, generally good for defense against magickal attack.

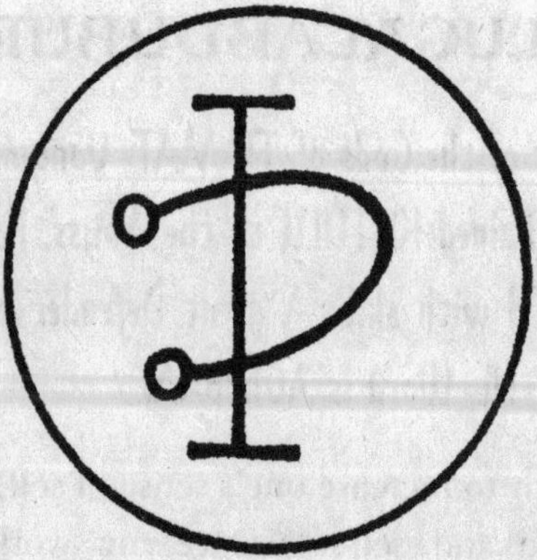

37.

The Thirty-Seventh Name is PAGALGUENNA.

Possessor of Infinite Intelligence, and determines the nature of things not yet made, and of spirits not yet created, and knows the strength of the Gods. His Word is ARRABABAAL.

An arcane spirit, surely, who can reveal to you the wisdom of taking certain courses of action in your life or business or personal affairs. Can show you where a certain plan of action might lead you if followed through the way you have it set up.

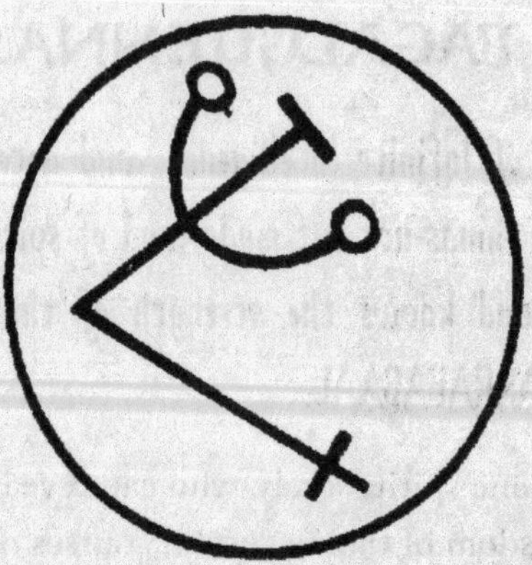

38.

The Thirty-Eighth Name is LUGALDURMAH.

The Lord of Lofty Places, Watcher of the Skies and all that travels therein. Naught traverses the starry element, but that this Power is aware. His Word is ARATAAGARBAL.

Increases psychic awareness, even in those who claim they have no ESP. Trains the mind in picking up subconscious signals from others, forewarns of precognition. Good for astrologers and diviners, or to invoke before going to see a reader or astrologer to insure a true reading.

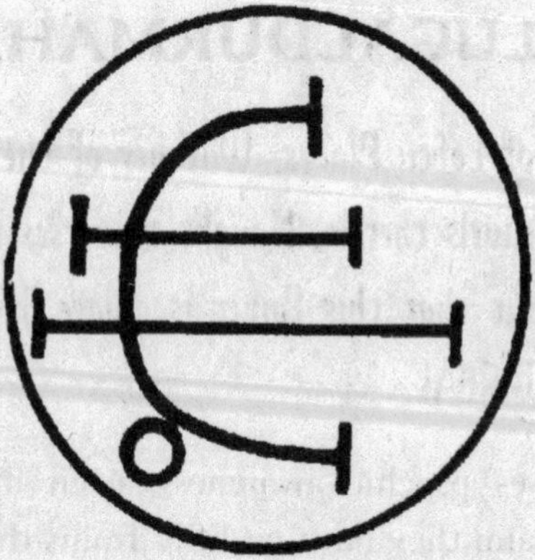

39.
The Thirty-Ninth Name is ARANUNNA.

Giver of Wisdom, Counselor to our Father, ENKI, Knower of the Magickal Covenant and of the Laws and of the Nature of the Gates. His Word is ARAMANNGI.

The Magickal Covenant is descriptive of the uneasy truce that exists between the forces of Good and Evil—or, if you will, the Ancient Ones and the Elder Gods, both alien life forms which somehow contributed to the birth of the human race and which now vie for superiority over us. The Gates refer to the process of self-initiation contained in the NECRONOMICON. This is a useful Spiritual Guide for those involved in any form of occult self-initiation, for ARANUNNA sometimes acts as a Teacher.

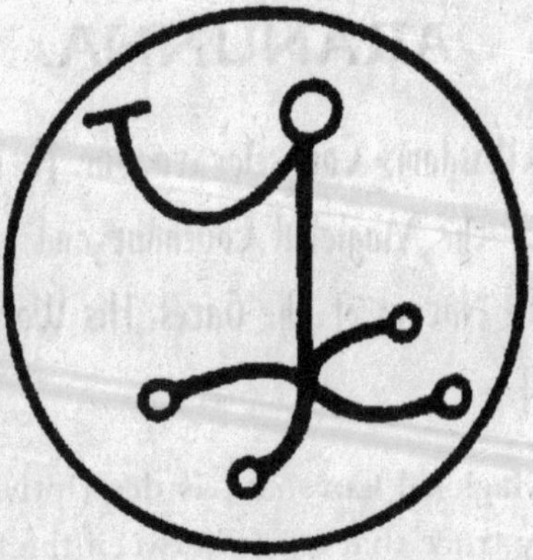

40.
The Fortieth Name is DUMUDUKU.

Possessor of the Wand of Lapis Lazuli, Knower of the Secret Name and the Secret Number. May not reveal these to thee, but may speak of other things, equally marvellous. His Word is ARATAGIGI.

An awesome Force, difficult to summon. Of little practical use, it would seem, except that the "other things, equally marvellous" can sometimes be quite useful! Not to be attempted until after you have mastered at least ten or twelve of the others. Once summoned, DUMUDUKU is difficult to hold for very long.

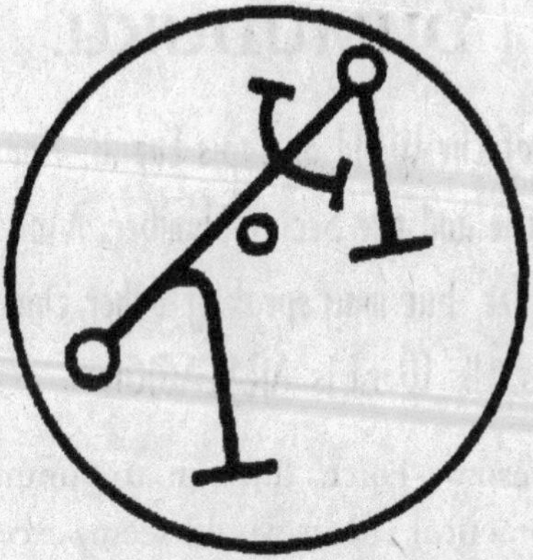

41.
The Forty-First Name is LUGALANNA.

The Power of the Eldest of the Elder Ones, possesses the secret knowledge of the world when the Ancient Ones and the Elder Ones were One. Knows the Essence of the Ancient Ones and where it might be found. His Word is BALDIKHU.

Increases your own power, especially your magick ability. Assists in finding your own True Will—a most necessary step in becoming proficient in all magick. Also has the uncanny ability to help you remember your past lives and other incarnations.

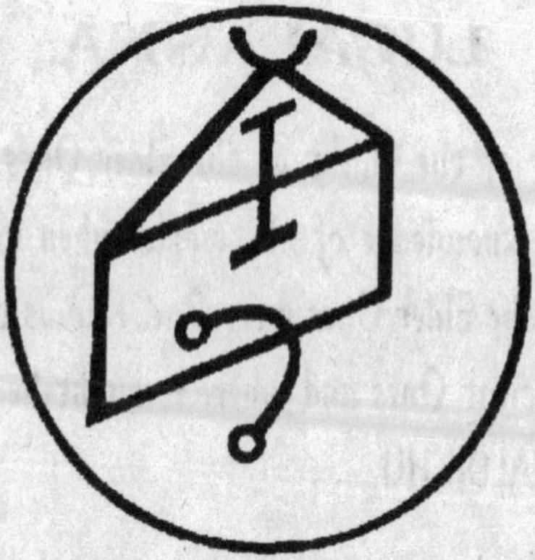

42.
The Forty-Second Name is LUGALUGGA.

Knows the Essences of all Spirits, of the Dead and the Unborn, and the Starry and the Earthly, and the Spirits of the Air and the Spirits of the Wind as well. Which things he may tell thee, and thou wilt grow in wisdom. His Word is ZIDUR.

Enables one to work magick with greater ease and speed, but also to divine the Truth in any given situation, to sense the reality behind the false-fronts of personal behavior in others, to know immediately when you are being deceived, or when others are deceiving themselves. For the magician, this Spirit gives excellent information concerning the art of Magick itself, and how the Spirits may best be summoned.

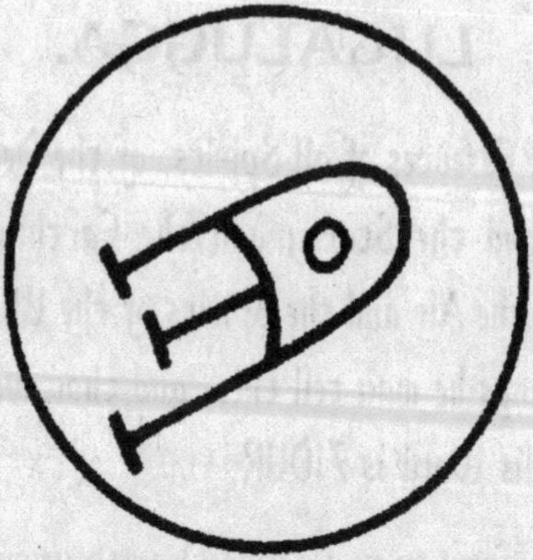

43.

The Forty-Third Name is IRKINGU.

This is the Power that laid capture to the Commander of the forces of the Ancient Ones, KINGU, Mighty Demon, that MARDUK might lay hold of him and, with its blood, create the Race of Men and seal the Covenant. His Word is BARERIMU.

This Spirit can also give knowledge of past lives and incarnations, because it was there at the time of the creation of the human race, and knows of its origins through the Blood and how the Demon KINGU was captured. When invoking this Spirit, meditate for awhile quietly before you close the circle, looking meanwhile into a smooth, polished surface like a mirror or a crystal ball, and various images will arise that will tell you what you wish to know.

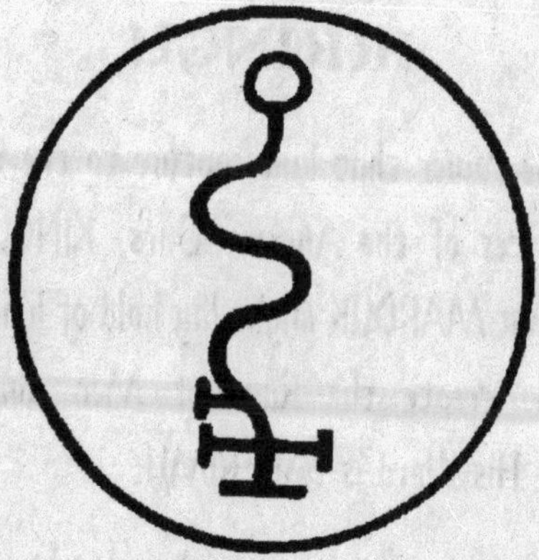

44.
The Forty-Fourth Name is KINMA.

Judge and Lord of the Gods, at whose name they quake in fear. That the Gods may not err, this Power was given to oversee their activities, should they be law-ful and within the nature of the Covenant, for the Gods are forgetful, and very far away. His Word is ENGAIGAL.

When all else fails, when your prayers and invocations come to nothing, when it seems as though God has forgotten you and abandoned you to your fate, when the situation seems hopeless with no chance of improvement, call on KINMA with all your heart and mind and soul. Empty yourself of your fear and loneliness in his presence, and he will carry your message to the throne of the Gods themselves.

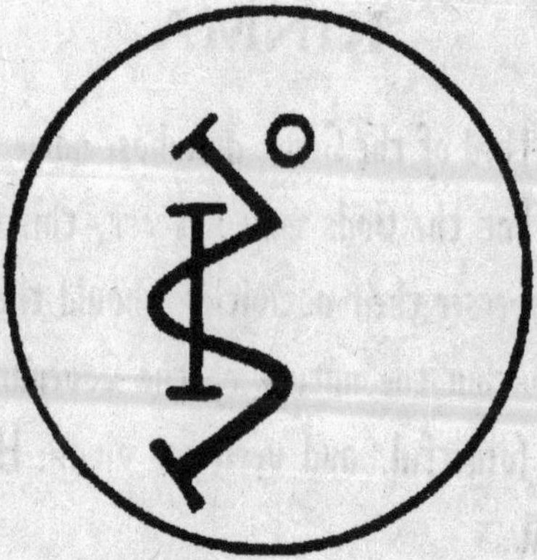

45.

The Forty-Fifth Name is ESIZKUR.

This Spirit possesses the knowledge of the length of Life of any man, even unto the plants and the demons and the Gods. He measureth all things, and knoweth the Space thereof. His Word is NENIGEGAL.

About this spirit we may not speak. He can be invoked at your own discretion, should you find such information desirable or necessary. A word of advice, though, from someone experienced in these matters. Do not ask from ESIZKUR knowledge of your own length of life. Unless you are prepared to deal with that information in a useful and productive way.

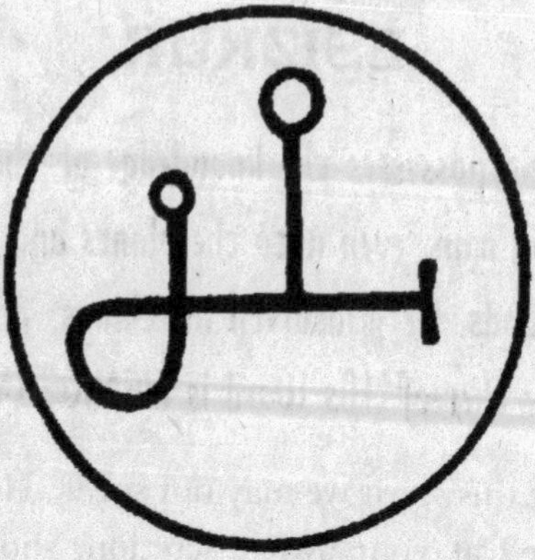

46.
The Forty-Sixth Name is GIBIL.

This Power has been given the Realm of the Fire and the Forge. He keepeth the sharp point of the Sword and the Lance, and giveth understanding in the working of metals. He also raises the Lightning that comes from the Earth, and maketh Swords to appear in the Sky. His Word is BAALAGNITARRA.

According to the esoteric teaching, this Spirit initiates the magician into the processes of self-knowledge, refining those base components of ourselves that remain secret even to us—or are revealed through the costly process of psychotherapy and analysis. Helps you to understand why you are the victim of passions and urges you cannot control—and how to eventually control them. Worth the trouble involved to invoke for the serious student.

47.
The Forty-Seventh Name is ADDU.

Raises storms that fill the entire heavens and causes the Stars to tremble and the very Gates of the IGIGI to shake in their stead. Can fill the skies with his brightness, even in the darkest hour of the night. His Word is KAKODAMMU.

Sometimes it is too difficult to deal with a situation that involves a great many extenuating circumstances, the personal feelings of several people, which may be confused, for instance. The invocation of ADDU can dispel the confusion and the troubled feelings and help clear the air in a quick and dramatic fashion. In extreme cases ADDU can abruptly change the entire situation for the better by throwing a fast-moving random factor into the pattern that causes everything to change and dispel bad energy.

48.

The Forty-Eighth Name is ASHARRU.

Knower of the Treacherous Ways. Gives intelligence of the Future and also of things Past. Put the Gods in their courses and determined their cycles. His Word is BAXTANDABAL.

Gives information, but does not act on commands. An excellent Spirit to invoke before doing a card-reading or asking any question about the future. Has an uncanny way of getting to the heart of any matter put before him.

49.
The Forty-Ninth Name is NEBIRU.

This is the Spirit of the Gate of MARDUK. Manages all things in their ways, and moves the crossings of the stars after the fashion known to the Chaldeans. His Word is DIRGIRGIRI.

To be invoked when you feel a need for order and pattern in your life, or someone else's. When a sense of security and safety is desired or needed, of comfort and well-being, and of peace.

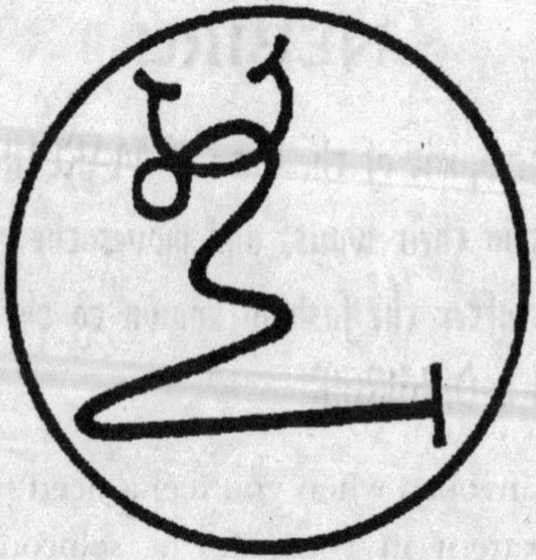

50.
The Fiftieth Name is NINNUAM.

This is the Power of MARDUK as Lord of All That Is, Judger of Judgments, Decider of Decisions, He Who Determines the Laws and the Reign of Kings. He may not be called, save at the destruction of a city or the death of a king. His Word is GASHDIG.

The warning should be observed scrupulously. "King," however, may be taken to mean also—besides heads of state and monarchs—corporation executives and religious leaders.

AFTERWORD

BY NOW you have been intrigued and mystified by the bizarre contents of this ancient and awesome occult text, and you may be wondering what possibilities the NECRONOMICON has in store for you. Does it really work?

Far from deriding such a skeptical attitude, might I say that it is the only attitude to take in regards to any occult service or textbook. We live in a scientific age, the age of space travel and nuclear energy, of genetic engineering and robots, of pocket calculators and home computers. And, in the midst of all this technological achievement, there appears like a ghost from the Eldritch past, the NECRONOMICON. In the age of push-button commands issued from sleek terminals in sterile, air-conditioned computer rooms there comes a book of incantation and exorcism. Among the bespectacled, distracted technicians, programmers and engineers, stands the stark and faintly terrifying figure of the Mad Arab. The juxtaposition is incredible. What does it mean? What does it portend?

We have not yet been able to give a computer the gift of thought. From the most primitive, hand-held calculator to the massive consoles in research centers around the world, all the computer can really do is: compute. People are the only machines that are capable of thought, of creativity, of art and of love. That which sets us apart from the computers is what draws us towards the NECRONOMICON, for it speaks to our spirit, and speaks of dangers our spirit may face in attempting to unleash untold, untested cosmic forces upon our planet and ourselves. You don't have to believe in the religion of the Sumerians in order to work the miracles of the NECRONOMICON, for it was the magick of the NECRONOMICON that gave spawn to the religion of Sumer. You merely have to believe in yourself. Give yourself—that part of you that you know is better than any machine, any space-shuttle, any computer—a chance at succeeding where others have failed. Don't merely believe in the NECRONOMICON. Try it. Not once, but several times. Give it a thoroughly scientific battery of tests.

And then sit back and enjoy the show.

Good hunting.

Stoop not down, therefore,
Unto the Darkly-Splendid
World,
Wherin continually lieth
A faithless Depth
And Hades wrapped in clouds,
Delighting in unintelligible
Images,
Precipitous, winding,
A black, ever-rolling Abyss
Ever espousing a Body
Unluminous
Formless
And Void.

The Chaldean Oracles of Zoroaster